THE DAY OF THE SON

A Revelation of God's heart

MARTIN OSSEI

LIFE AND SUCCESS PUBLISHING
www.abookinsideyou.com

Copyright © Martin Ossei 2016

All rights reserved. No part of this publication may be produced, distributed, or transmitted in any form or by any means, including photocopying, recording, or other electronic or mechanical methods, without the prior written permission of the publisher, or except in the case of brief quotations embodied in critical reviews and certain other noncommercial uses permitted by copyright law.
For permission requests, write to the publisher, addressed "Attention: Permissions Coordinator" at the email address below

Life and Success Media Ltd
email info@abookinsideyou.com
www.abookinsideyou.com

This book is sold subject to the condition that it may not be resold or otherwise issued except in its original binding.
The CIP catalogue record for this book is available from the British Library. British Library Cataloguing-in-Publishing Data.
All quotations are from the Holy Bible New King James and New International version unless otherwise stated.

ISBN: 978-1-907402-87-6

Cover design & layout by **mia**design.com

TABLE OF CONTENTS

FOREWORD 5

INTRODUCTION 9

Chapter One: IN THE BEGINNING GOD 13

Chapter Two: GIFT OF THE LAND 19

Chapter Three: THE DAY OF THE SON 31

Chapter Four: MANY SONS 47

Chapter Five: THE CROSS IS THE HEART OF THE MATTER 57

Chapter Six: THE BLOOD OF JESUS 71

Chapter Seven: THE BREATH OF GOD 81

Chapter Eight: THE REAL YOU 99

Chapter Nine: VISION AND BOUNDARIES 111

Chapter Ten: CHALLENGES AND VICTORIES 125

Chapter Eleven: LAST MAN STANDING 131

Chapter 12: LAST WORD 135

FOREWORD

Martin Ossei is one of a generation of expatriate church leaders who have established new church congregations in urban areas, in his case North London, UK. When you meet him, what strikes you immediately is his radiant warmth and passionate enthusiasm for the Christian Faith he lives and proclaims. It is this same warmth, passion and enthusiasm that he pours into this book. Every page bursts with excitement at God's great works, making it both inspirational and easy to read.

Martin grew up in Ghana as a regular churchgoer. He was familiar with church life and its routines. However everything changed when Jesus came into his life. He longs to see others set free from empty religious ritual, as he has been. A wind of freshness is blown into well-known Bible accounts as Martin takes us from the wonder of our individual creation, through our rebellion, and on to 'The Day of the Son'. This is the act for all time when God sent Jesus to rescue us from all our sins.

Central to God's wonderful purposes is the cross where Jesus bore our sins and defeated Satan's power of death. The power of Jesus' blood shed takes us right out of Satan's clutches. In chapter after chapter there is a high sense of drama in the victory achieved for us in the spiritual realms.

Beyond all this, every believer is to be filled with the promised Holy Spirit. Just as God breathed life into us at creation, so now the Spirit breathes into us the very life of God. With supernatural power amongst the believers, the Church experiences healings and wonders, and the children of God stand tall and full of light to bring change in the land.

Martin gathers believers from many churches with a vision for Harlesden and Brent in North London. With steadfast prayer and with courage to take on every battle, he offers a vision for a better world, and a God shaped world. This will be The Day of the Son.

Rt. Rev. Graham Dow
Bishop of Carlisle

Frannie's Review

This is a book which will appeal to those as yet still outside of the Kingdom, as well as to those who have entered in.

Martin traces the revelation of God's heart from the very beginning, a very useful exercise for us all to undertake from time to time. It is good to be reminded of and to rehearse our salvation history.

I very much concur with the outline of gradual transformation in the local region that he portrays. It was my privilege to be part of this process in the early 1990's. It was a hard graft but our unity, persistence and determination had its reward as we witnessed the structural changes that occurred, to the benefit of the local community at that time.

Read this book and pass it on, especially to loved ones, friends and others within your sphere of influence. They will not only be blessed by this book, but will also have the opportunity to meet Him, whom the author of this book acknowledges as Lord of all.

Francesca Cornu Fleming
Director, Gateway Ministries
Gosport, UK.

INTRODUCTION

When that young man questioned me about the reality of God and the necessity of faith in Jesus Christ, my heart went out to him. I understood where he was coming from. I had been in his position. He was searching for truth. Truth ends all searching. I thank God that the light of God invaded my darkness and brought revelation of the truth. The joy of knowing the heart and ways of God fills me with much gratitude. Each day as the Holy Spirit reveals new things. I can only shout, "Praise God!"

Coming from a religious background and having been in church all my life, my encounter with Jesus Christ had to be more than the rituals and traditions I was used to. I could say all the prayers and sing all the songs yet I was empty inside. My addictions, my lusts and negative emotions held me hostage and condemned me to a life of anxiety and unfulfilled dreams.

Thank God I met with Jesus Christ outside the rituals of religion and He has transformed my life by giving me insight into what I originally thought were untouchable mysteries of God. I have been set free indeed. Who the Son sets free is free indeed. I was waiting for my liberation and I got it. I am now on an assignment to see others set free.

My desire is that this book will not only set you free but set you on the path of becoming a fulfilled worker in God's world. I asked God to help me write a book that will be helpful to both young and mature believers as well as unbelievers . The Day of the Son is the result of this quest. God's heart and your place in God's plan is the theme of the book. You have a definite and secure place in God's plan. It is a generally accepted fact that we as humans are not operating anywhere near our full potential. No scientific discovery or progress in inventions has succeeded in getting rid of this grim assessment. Does the maker of man have a secret the world is not aware of? Read on.

My prayer is that this revelation of the Father, Son, Holy Spirit and your place in the Trinity, will not just make interesting reading but will transform your life. Enjoy reading.

CHAPTER ONE

In the Beginning, God

The authority of the very first line of the bible is amazing.

"In the beginning God created the heavens and the earth."
Genesis 1:1

This declaration of truth which hits your heart like a thunderbolt is characteristic of the living God, wherever he appeared. He speaks and settles it. When Jesus spoke, He settled it. He made statements like, " I am the light of the world;""I am the bread of life;""I am the resurrection and the life;""I am the way, the truth and the life." His statements were definite statements of authority. No wonder His disciple Peter shouted: *"You are the Christ, the Son of the living God"* in *Matthew 16:16.*

It is this virtue in Jesus that made the messengers of the pharisees and chief priests remark in *John 7:46* that they never heard any man speak like Him. These officers had been sent to arrest him by the rulers of the day. They could not touch Him and had to return to their masters without Him. The truth that came from Jesus had overcome every fear they had of the consequences of their failure to carry out the assignment.

Truth has authority.
Truth is powerful and will always win.
The victory of a lie is only temporary.
The eternal nature of God is linked to the fact that He is true.

With great authority, God commanded light into being. He created day and night, the sun and the moon, the sky and the sea, all trees and all animals by the power of His Word. *Genesis 1:1-25* is God's power and authority at display. It is interesting to note the change in language and tempo in Genesis 1:26 when God says

" Let us make man in our image, according to our likeness; let them have dominion .."

The language here seems to slow down, expressing a thought. The military precision in the language of the previous verses changes. He sounds like seeking some form of agreement here. Creating man in His own image and likeness and giving him dominion over part of His creation is the language of love. We can only imagine the sense of pride and elation as God set about creating man in His own image and likeness. The joy of loving parents on the birth of their first child cannot be compared to this. God has a big heart so His emotions must be big.

It is great degradation to put man in the same class as animals. The profound verse of *Genesis 2:7* tells us that though God formed man from the dust of the earth, He performed an intimate act of breathing into his nostrils, thereby giving him the very life of God.

Man without God is as the dust of the earth. The Hebrew word translated dust could also be translated rubbish. God did not breath into any animal. No animal has the capacity to be saved. The theory of evolution is ignorant philosophy parading as science. Many scientists have bought into this lie confirming John 3:19

"And this is the condemnation, that the light has come into the world and men loved darkness rather than light because their deeds were evil."

"If my mind can't think it, I can't accept it" is the flawed wisdom of the proud. Man's brains are made of the dust. It is only the breath of God that can enhance its quality. The capacity of our brains is limited. The brain can be damaged and not function properly. I thank God for my brain. I will develop my brain as best I can and enjoy this gift of God. I also have total trust in the supernatural breath of God that enables me to perform beyond my human brain capacity. Paul summarises this thought beautifully in 1 Corinthians 2:16

"For who has known the mind of the Lord that he may instruct Him? But we have the mind of Christ."

The book of Job in the Bible is in the main about a man desiring some answers. Life has dealt him a blow he cannot understand. He has done his best to serve God but he does not really know God. When unexpected disaster hits his life, he seeks explanation. His wife is so frustrated with the situation, she asks Job to curse God and die. His friends offer their understanding of the situation. The people around Job including Job himself have their minds working overtime. God intervenes and admonishes Job and his friends for trying to give counsel without knowledge. **True knowledge is the exclusive preserve of the living God.** He decides who he shares it with. He created man for the purpose of sharing His creation:

"Let us make man in our image, according to Our likeness; let them have dominion over the fish of the sea, over the birds of the air, and over the cattle, over all the earth and over every creeping thing that creeps on the earth (Genesis 1:26)."

In the last chapters of the book of Job, God begins to question Job about things that are beyond Job's understanding. Questions about how the foundation of the earth was laid; about who commands the morning; what springs feed the sea; about mountain goats and the whole complex nature of creation. Job admits in the second verse of the final chapter of Job:

"I have uttered what I did not understand. Things too wonderful for me which I did not know."

God's creation is amazing: The planets, natural rock formations, the beauty of the sky at night, animal life, great water falls and the like. There are amazing natural wonders to behold wherever you go. Many are ready to pay huge amounts of money to own some of God's creation depicted on canvas. We haven't seen anything yet as this earth is just a tiny part of God's creation. Every country in the world has its own natural attractions created by God. God wants to reveal a lot more of Himself and the Heavens to us. Let us receive Him.

CHAPTER 2
Gift of the Land

The wedding invitation from my old school friend stated that it was going to be an African traditional wedding. An African traditional wedding consists of the groom's family bringing gifts and dowry to the bride's family. If the gifts are accepted, there is a blessing and in some cases, exchange of rings and the marriage is settled. Although these traditional weddings tend to be slightly different in style depending on which part you came from, the core programme was the same. I had attended quite a few of these weddings. What happened at my friends wedding was however unexpected. He had a fully robed voodoo priest standing in to officiate. I found this strange as I knew my friend as a nominal Christian. I had heard of witches sent to disrupt Christian services. I decided to do the opposite here by standing as an agent of God, praying under my breath, to disrupt this open manifestation of the occult, for the sake of my friend. At the end of the ceremony, I had the opportunity to have a discussion with my friend. Though highly educated with a highly educated wife, my friend believed that many roads led to God. I asked him what his road was. His answer was a confusion of God in heaven and the earth being a female deity, supposedly God's wife. The discussion led to how Europe used religion to subjugate Africa and ended up on the issue of racism. He confessed to me that he did not really believe in voodoo but it was his form of a political protest. This is a classic case of *"My people are destroyed for lack of knowledge" (Hosea 4:6).*

Rebellion is the source of all idolatry. The first commandment God gave Israel was

"I am the Lord your God ... You should have no other Gods before me."

God drove the nations before Israel because the nations served other gods. When you disobey God, you are a rebel and you take after your father Satan who was the first rebel. The prophet Samuel tells King Saul of Israel after he had disobeyed God:

"For rebellion is as the sin of witchcraft And stubbornness as iniquity and idolatry (1 Samuel 15:23)."

The subject of land was important to my friend. In the first place, the earth was so important that it is regarded as the mother of mankind. He was also offended by the colonisation of Africa as, according to him, through deception Europe had stolen the land of Africa. Many wars in the world today are fought over land. The Israeli - Palestinian issue is a good example of such conflicts. There are young people fighting "post code" gang wars in London. They ban other young people from other post codes coming into their "territory". These are young people many of whom are still at home with their parents. They fiercely guard their illegal territories. Land is important to them

Right from the beginning of creation, God's gift to man was the land. In Genesis 1:26, not only did God have a plan to give man dominion over the entire earth, in verse 27, He created man in his image and likeness; and in verse 28:

"Then God blessed them and God said to them 'Be fruitful and multiply, fill the earth and subdue it, have dominion over the fish of the sea, over the birds of the air and over every living thing that moves on the earth."

God is in the sharing business. In the beginning, God made the heavens and the earth. By the end of that chapter, he had already created a man with whom he was sharing his creation. **He gave man complete control of the earth.** When man disobeyed God by seeking knowledge outside the knowledge of God, he lost his position of dominion over the earth. The desire of man when he disobeyed God in the Garden of Eden was to have complete knowledge and dominion. He already possessed these in God.

The Bible says it was the habit of God to have a stroll in the garden in the cool of the day. All Adam needed to do was ask and God would answer and tell him all he wanted to know. One of the promises of God to those who obey Him is:

"If you walk in My statutes and keep My commandments, and perform them, then I will give you rain in its season, the land shall yield its produce and the trees of the field shall yield their fruit. Your threshing shall last till the time of vintage, and the vintage shall last till the time of sowing; you shall eat your bread to the full, and dwell in your land safely. I will give peace in the land, and you shall lie down, and none will make you afraid; I will rid the land of evil beasts, and the sword will not go through your land." Leviticus 26:3-6.

Satan hates God and hates man with a passion because he knows God loves man with a passion. The aim of Satan is to destroy man to hurt God. He counters every move of God. He uses deception and lies. He deceived Adam and Eve to eat of the forbidden tree and succeeded in cutting them away from God. Adam and Eve could have said 'No' and countered Satan's deceptive words with God's truth. In this war of words, who would you choose to believe and obey. Adam and Eve chose to believe and obey Satan and ended up being slaves to their own possession. In the end, the enemy who told them they would be like God if they rebelled against God is the same one who put fear in them by whispering to them that they were naked. When God called out to Adam, Adam hid himself because he felt naked. God's question to Adam in *Genesis 3:11 was:*

"Who told you that you were naked?"

There were only two voices Adam and Eve could respond to at the time, God and Satan. God did not tell him he was naked so it was Satan who did.

Adams reward for disobeying God and obeying Satan was:

"Cursed is the ground for your sake; In toil you shall eat of it all the days of your life. Both thorns and thistles it shall bring forth for you. And you shall eat the herb of the field. In the sweat of your face you shall eat bread till you return to the ground. For out of it you were taken; For dust you are, And to dust you shall return." Genesis 3:17-19.

The same land that Adam had power to subdue and dominate was now going to be a source of much suffering and toil to him. The land would no longer respond to him. In fact the land of opportunity had turned into his grave. Adam was driven away from the Garden of Eden and an angel was placed there to protect the Garden from Adam. Adam had made a choice to be like God knowing good from evil so he had become his own god. He now had to fend for himself in a world he knew very little about. He was in a tragic situation: No land, no possession, no protection. This is compounded by a family tragedy as his son Cain kills his brother Abel out of envy. Where did envy come from? The sentence of Cain for this murder was that even when he worked the land, it would not respond fully. He would also be a fugitive and vagabond unable to settle. That was the curse hanging over mankind until Jesus paid the price for the sin of the world with His death.

The earth represents God's stability. No earthquake, volcanic eruption, mud slide, hurricane, tsunami or global warming can shake the earth off its foundation. The earth is solidly founded. Only God its maker can remove the foundation of the earth. Yes, what is impossible with any man is possible with God. In Revelation 21:1, John saw a new heaven and a new earth, as the old earth and heaven had passed away.

The earth represents God's fruitfulness (provision). Animals and trees are produced from the earth. The earth produces food. It also produces the raw material for most of the inventions of man. The Garden of Eden did not only contain fruit trees and all sorts of animals, it also contained rivers and valuable precious metals. *Read Genesis 2:8-14.* Part of man was made from the earth. Man was not made from just the earth. God's plan in making man, as we saw in Genesis 1:26 was to make man in his image according to his likeness. Man's assignment from creation is to rule the earth. This is why God breathed into man after forming him from the dust of the earth. **Every man without the breath of God is incomplete.**

Incomplete man can never fulfil the assignment of the rulership of the earth. No one can claim true ownership of any land unless given to him by God.

"The creation waits in eager expectation for the sons of God to be revealed "- Romans 8:19

In a world without God's order, the strong possess the land. You read about several wars in the Old Testament. It looks as if all the kings of the nations in the Bible did was to plan for war. They sought to defeat other nations, take over their lands and collect tributes from them. This meant that though you worked on the land, you gave out the fruit of your labour as tribute to a stronger king or master. This was the motivation behind empires of old. Nebuchadnezzar of Babylon, Alexander of Greece, Caesars of Rome were strong men with great armies who forcibly took over lands. This is the whole idea behind colonisation. Through force or influence of money, ownership of lands change. In today's world, brute force is generally condemned but the use of money has become generally acceptable. **The right heirs must arise and take possession of the land.** This means you, if you have accepted God's invitation and become part of his family.

God's land will be possessed by God's chosen people. God began to cultivate a special relationship with Abraham. He was invited to leave his country to a land that God would show him. If Abraham was obedient, he would enjoy what God intended for man from the beginning. If Abraham would leave the place of struggle which he called home, God Himself would give him special land and much favour. Abraham obeyed God and that land *"as far as his eyes could see"* became Abraham's and his descendants' forever. Although Abraham was never crowned king in the way of the world, he was a king in all other respects because God was with him. He defended kings, defeated strong kings in battle, had favour with the kings of Egypt and Philistine, communed with God and could intercede on behalf of nations.

Abraham's gift from God was the land of Canaan. No one can take this land from Abraham and his seed. Though the seed of Abraham had to go through the training ground of Egypt for four hundred years, the land was waiting for them. They came back under the leadership of Moses and Joshua to possess their land. As long as they were obedient, no one could stand before them.

God performed miracle after miracle to ensure the fulfilment of His covenant with Abraham.

Whatever promise God has given to you, He will do miracle after miracle to ensure its fulfilment. Are you living in the land of God's promise? Do not be shaken if you are still dwelling in tents. You can still exercise the authority of a king. No enemy can take your God given land from you. The pretenders shall be defeated. This was God's promise to Israel through the prophet Isaiah:

"For Zion's sake I will not hold My peace,
And for Jerusalem's sake I will not rest,
Until her righteousness goes forth as brightness,
And her salvation as a lamp that burns.
The Gentiles shall see your righteousness,

And all kings your glory. You shall be called by a new name, Which the mouth of the Lord will name.

Isaiah 62:1-2

CHAPTER 3
The Day of the Son

Trying to beat God at anything is a fool's venture. He started everything, created all things, knows everything including the thoughts of men. He sees everything and is all powerful. Why would anyone think of taking God on? Ignorance. Saul (Paul) was so incensed with the early Church that he punished himself with rage, moving from city to city with the avowed aim of destroying this new movement of Christians. **You cannot kill what God has given life to.** He ended up becoming an avowed member of this movement and one of its leading proponents. The Bible is full of accounts of people who have done a u turn and acknowledged Jehovah God as the great God of the universe.

A friend of mine, who raged at born again Christians especially his wife, and was like Paul in his intensity of hatred for Christians, told me he found himself knocking on a Pastor's door. When the pastor opened the door and asked him why he was there, he did not know why he was there. He had ridden his motor bike to the pastor's house after a night out partying. He had not planned to. A motor bike angel had probably taken over the steering. He sank on his knees and gave his life to the Lord. He is now a deacon in a full gospel Church.

When Satan deceived man in the garden of Eden. His elation, if he had any, was very short lived. In Genesis 3:15, God pronounces a sentence on Satan:

"I will put enmity between you and the woman and between your seed and her Seed. He shall bruise your head and you shall bruise His heel."

God set a plan in motion by which the seed or son of the woman was going to crush the head of Satan. Satan's abode would be under the heel of the Son. The above pronouncement in the Garden of Eden would be the first announcement of the assignment of Jesus Christ to the world and to Satan. Satan knows God and knew that He would fulfil His promise. This announcement provoked different reactions from Satan and man. Satan was furious and sought to destroy all men. Man awaited the arrival of the Son for his deliverance.

In Exodus 1:16, Pharaoh the king of Egypt gave the order for all new born males to be killed. In Matthew 2:16 king Herod of Judea gave the order for all boys up to the age of two in his domain to be slaughtered. Both kings were afraid of losing authority over their land. Influenced by Satan, they were trying to prevent the fulfilment of the curse spoken over Satan.

Illegitimate rulers live in constant fear of being overthrown.

Injustice cannot be protected forever.
The true justice of God shall prevail in the end.

"And there is no creature hidden from His sight, but all things are naked and open to the eyes of Him to whom we must give account." Hebrews 4:13

Pharaoh killed as many as he could but he could not kill Moses. Herod killed as many as he could but could not kill Jesus. Jesus and Moses had an assignment of God to perform and it was done. You shall perform God's assignment in your hands. The enemy has no chance of stopping you.

The greatest enemy to the true heir is the pretender. The true heir is unruffled and is not desperate. The true heir manifests the glory of God:

*"And the Word became flesh and dwelt among us, and we beheld His glory, the glory as of the only begotten of the Father, **full of grace and truth**." John 1:14.*

Saul pursued David all over the place in order to kill him, yet David maintained his dignity and even when he had opportunity to kill Saul, he did not. Although David had already been anointed to be king, he was not desperate for it. He trusted in God and His timing. God loved him. He fulfilled his destiny. He became a good and strong king over Israel and consolidated God's gift to Israel the land of Canaan flowing with milk and honey. He silenced the enemies all around and was able to give a good inheritance to his son Solomon - a land of peace.

Where is the Son?

The manifestation of the Son was essential for the deliverance and peace of mankind. Israel enjoyed the fruit of God's covenant with their father Abraham. God was faithful to His word and brought them to the land He promised Abraham. God had told them that if Israel obeyed Him, He would be their God and they would be His peculiar people above all nations. When Israel walked with God, they were invincible. David was a good king and brought some deliverance to his nation. Yet the promise of God was not completely fulfilled. Everyone waited for the Son. They wanted that special deliverance God had promised.

God had promised that through Abraham's seed, the whole world would be blessed. He had promised David that his seed shall build him a house and his kingdom shall last forever (1 Chronicles 17:4-14). All these were references to the coming Deliverer. God used the prophets to prophesy about the coming of the Son. One of the most profound prophesies being Isaiah 9:6,7:

" For unto us a Child is born, Unto us a Son is given;
And the government will be upon His shoulder.
And His name will be called
Wonderful, Counsellor, Mighty God,
Everlasting Father, Prince of Peace.
Of the increase of His government and peace,
There will be no end,
Upon the throne of David and over His kingdom,
To order it and establish it with judgment and justice
From that time forward, even forever.
The zeal of the Lord of hosts will perform this."

Isaiah had prophesied earlier in chapter 7:14 that a virgin shall conceive and bear a Son and shall call His name Immanuel (meaning God with us). Everyone was waiting. The prophetess Anna sensed the time was near and stayed in the house of God in continued intercession for the arrival of the Son. The devout man Simeon had a promise from God that he would see the Son

(Deliverer, Messiah, Christ) before his death and he was glad to see him and praised God for it.

One day, as shepherds watched their flock at night, Heaven sent messengers (angels) to announce to them that the Son, the deliverer had been born in Bethlehem. They announced that God would be glorified in Heaven and peace and goodwill would be to all men. Confidence in the Word of God had paid off. The legitimate heir had been born. Watch out! imposters and pretenders, the true Son and heir had arrived..

"Now I say that the heir, as long as he is a child, does not differ at all from a slave, though he is master of all, but is under guardians and stewards until the time appointed by the father." Galatians 4:1,2

When the appointed time of the Father came, Jesus Christ, the expected Son, walked to the the River Jordan to be baptised by John the prophet of God who had been sent as His fore runner and announcer. John bore witness of the Son as he announced publicly that this was the expected one, the Son of God. Immediately after Jesus' baptism, the Holy Spirit, the breath of God, descended on Jesus like a dove and the voice of the Father announced:

"You are my beloved Son in whom am well pleased." Mark 1:11,

Again in Matthew 17:5, after the Father shows Jesus in His glory to His three close associates, Peter, John and James, He announces to them:

"This is My beloved Son in whom I am well pleased. Hear Him."

The day of the Son had come. Satan had not been able to stop it. Satan tried his best to stop the godly destiny earmarked for us, but what God had purposed had surely come to pass. As Jesus embarked on the fulfilment of His assignment, Satan personally came against him. He used his family, townsmen, the priests and the rulers of the time against him. All to no avail. **What God had started, He would complete.** The Son of God was manifest that He may crush the head of Satan.

Assignment of the Son

Jesus preached to the people that the kingdom of God is here. He taught the people to pray, to love, to be humble and trust God as their father. He healed the sick as a demonstration of His authority over the devil and as a sign of what to expect in God's kingdom. **The main assignment of Jesus Christ was to crush Satan and free mankind from the prison of the devil.**

"Inasmuch then as the children have partaken of flesh and blood, He Himself likewise shared in the same, that through death He might destroy him who had the power of death, that is, the devil, and release those who through fear of death were all their lifetime subject to bondage." Hebrews 2:14,15

Jesus took on Satan's greatest weapon - death - and defeated him there. Jesus emptied Himself of all His privileges and humbled Himself to death on the cross. He defeated Satan's dreaded weapon of death. He rose from the dead. He could confidently declare to John after His resurrection:

"I am He who lives, and was dead, and behold, I am alive forevermore. Amen. And I have the keys of Hades and of Death." Revelation 1:18.

The Son has come and fulfilled His assignment. Satan's head is completely crushed. To everyone who receives this truth, you can enjoy a life of victory over Satan. Colossians 2:15 says Jesus disarmed principalities and powers, making a public spectacle of them and triumphing in it.

To ignore the work of the Cross is to refuse the most valuable free gift you can ever have.

The price has been paid. Satan is defeated. There is no reason for anyone to continue paying the price of sin.

The chains are broken. If we will rise, we will see them fall off.

The chains of sin, sickness, lack, poverty, depression and hopelessness are broken.

Rise up and see strength return to your legs. Jesus paid the price for you to have strong legs.

The Rights of the Son

The Jews sought to kill Jesus not because He said He was God but because He said He was the son of God:

"Therefore the Jews sought all the more to kill Him, because He not only broke the Sabbath, but also said that God was His Father, making Himself equal with God." John 5:18

What belongs to the Father belongs to the Son. The Father and Son are equal. The son is the natural heir of the father. If the earth belongs to the Father then it naturally belongs to the Son, especially the obedient Son. When you are recognised as a son, you are not only a bona fide member of the family but you have attained full rights and privileges as well as responsibilities of an heir. The son's responsibility is to take care of the family business, promote and protect it from predators. What is the Son of God's responsibility? To promote and protect His Father's property and kingdom. What are His privileges? All that belong to the Father belong to the Son. The Son has ownership of all created things and has power to create.

"He is the image of the invisible God, the firstborn over all creation. For by Him all things were created that are in heaven and that are on earth, visible and invisible, whether thrones or dominions or principalities or powers. All things were created through Him and for Him." Colossians 1:15,16.

The Son has the authority of the Father and operates in His name. He has the authority to take back all stolen items and rightfully restore all illegalities. He has the power to drive out all squatters and bring the building back to its original beauty and purpose. Satan's deception in the Garden of Eden had separated man from God and lost man the privilege of sonship, the entitlement to rulership of this earth. Satan has therefore unlawfully controlled the world through fear and manipulation. He seems to wield his power through various economic and political systems, businesses, schools, media and the like. **Man is no match for Satan without the Breath of God.** Satan is frightfully aware that the manifestation of the son marks the end of his deception. His plan has always been to prevent the manifestation of the son.

The Anointed One

After Jesus was baptised in the Jordan where His identity was revealed by both John the baptiser and God the Father, He was tempted by Satan himself. Unlike Adam, He overcame this temptation with distinction. How did He overcome Satan? By repeating the Word of God to Satan. He used the expression "It is written" three times against the three temptations of Satan. Satan had no way around Jesus as Jesus stood on the Word of God. "It is written" is significant because it also means "it is settled. "This means God has not just said it, He has written it. The Bible tells us that God did not only give commands to Israel but He also wrote the commands on stone tablets so it would be remembered and taught through the generations (Exodus 24:12). Jesus response was admonishing Satan thus: "Can't you read the Word of God that He has written in stone?" Jesus was not on the defensive. **He boldly confronted Satan with God's Word as the son must do.** In Luke 4:8, He commands Satan to get behind him. In other words, Jesus was telling Satan: "I have an assignment to fulfil, don't stand in my way." Every son of God must rebuke the devil out of his way. He has no choice but to obey because he is a pretender with no authority except you give him one.

After Jesus had overcome the temptations of Satan, the Bible says Jesus returned in the power of the Spirit to Galilee, his home region. If Adam had silenced the devil in the Garden of Eden, he would have grown in stature and confidence towards his God given assignment. The opposition can only look on fearfully as you boldly sweep through with your assignment from God.

Jesus, armed with new boldness, was now ready to introduce Himself to the world as the Messiah (Christ, Anointed One, the Son). All Israel had been waiting for the Messiah. He chose a meeting in the Synagogue for this announcement. He read a prophecy from the book of Isaiah that spoke about the Messiah and his messianic assignment. He then closed the book, sat down and told His audience that He was the Messiah. Many in the audience could not handle this announcement. Of course, they were expecting the Anointed One but he was not going to come looking like one of them. They had known Jesus as a local boy and he was not much different from them. They got angry and were planning to kill Him. He was definitely out of His mind and a blasphemer. He looked too much like them. **The only difference between the ordinary man and the Son is the breath of God.** The scripture in Isaiah which Jesus quoted in Luke 4:18 begins with:

"The Spirit (breath) of the Lord is upon me, Because He has anointed Me."

Without the breath of God, man is dust and ordinary. With the breath of God, man can do what God can do.

CHAPTER 4

Many Sons

When the disciples of Jesus asked Him to teach them to pray, the first line he taught them to pray was:

"Our Father in Heaven" (Luke 11:2).

God loves to be a father. Many people are more comfortable seeing God as a master. He is the creator and owner of all things. That makes Him Lord and Master. But to merely view Him as Lord is not to know his heart. His Word is very clear that His desire is to be recognised as father. This is why when Jesus teaches to pray, he teaches us to address God as our father. God is the Lord and Master of the universe. He made them all and He has absolute control over His creation. His purpose for creating man however was to have sons. Creation is remarkable. Although we have only seen a tiny percentage of God's creation, what we see is amazing in terms of creativity and thought. In the midst of this awesome ability, one statement exposes the heart of God:

*"Then God said, "**Let Us make man in Our image, according to Our likeness**; let them have dominion over the fish of the sea, over the birds of the air, and over the cattle, over all the earth and over every creeping thing that creeps on the earth." Genesis 1:26.*

As much as the above scripture depicts God's kind and sharing heart, He is not sharing His creation with just anybody. He is sharing His creation with man whom He has created in His own image and likeness; someone whose appearance and attributes are just like His. He was creating a son for Himself. He gave us a physical body to enable us think, walk, talk, feel, see and hear like Him. He also breathed on us and gave us His breath that enabled the unseen part of our spirit and soul to have the capacity of functioning like Him. A father's love requires the response of a son's love. **A master demands the obedience of his servant; a father desires the love of his son**.

God had a scroll of Truth that no one was fit to open because not a single soul could pay the price needed to open this scroll. It took the Lion of the tribe of Judah, the Root of David, the Lamb that was slain, Jesus Christ, to open this scroll. God had to send His Son to be a seed to give Him many sons.

"But we see Jesus, who was made a little lower than the angels, for the suffering of death crowned with glory and honour, that He, by the grace of God, might taste death for everyone.

For it was fitting for Him, for whom are all things and by whom are all things, in bringing many sons to glory, to make the captain of their salvation perfect through sufferings. For both He who sanctifies and those who are being sanctified are all of one, for which reason He is not ashamed to call them brethren," Hebrews 2:9-11

Jesus has tasted death for every one. His death and resurrection marks a new era in the affairs of man and the world. The Bible tells us that Satan's weapon of intimidation is death. It also tells us that our punishment for separating ourselves from God is death. If Satan has used the fear of death to keep us in deception, then our deliverer needed to conquer death and do it openly for us to see. This He did openly on the cross of calvary. God made the defeat of Satan his personal responsibility. He accomplished this through the death of Jesus Christ on the Cross of Calvary. The price was paid for everyone who would respond to the invitation to be a son. We as men have to recognise and receive this victory. The enemy has no power over the son.

Who are the sons of God?

"He was in the world, and the world was made by him, and the world knew him not. He came unto his own, and his own received him not. But as many as received him, to them gave he power to become the sons of God, even to them that believe on his name: Which were born, not of blood, nor of the will of the flesh, nor of the will of man, but of God." John 1:10-13

What the Father can do, His Son Jesus can do. What Jesus can do, His brethren, the other sons can do. If you have received Jesus into your life, you are a son of God. To receive Jesus is to believe in the accomplished assignment of

His death and resurrection that defeated Satan's hold over us and to acknowledge His Lordship over all things. When you do this sincerely from your heart, you become a partaker in the sacrifice of Jesus Christ - His death and resurrection. When the people heard Peter preach in Acts 2 and were convicted in their hearts, they asked Peter what to do. Peter responded that they should repent, be baptised in the Name of Jesus Christ and they shall receive the Holy Spirit.

Repent is a decision we make to turn away from the world and all its deceptive attractions. **Be baptised** is an action we take to identify with the death and resurrection of our senior brother, Jesus Christ. Romans 6:3-4 tells us that when we are baptised into Christ Jesus, we are baptised into His death. We are buried with Him in baptism so that as He rose from the dead by the Father's glory, we will also walk in newness of life. **Receive the Holy Spirit** is a preparedness in our heart to receive the Breath of God. If you sincerely go through repentance and baptism, God is waiting to flood you with His Spirit. You therefore become a full fledged son of the living

God with all the benefits of a son of heaven. A son as used here is a title of position and not of gender. It simply means you are of the family and heir to the living God. It therefore applies to both men and women. Whosoever meets God's conditions will experience the wonderful inheritance of God. Let's not forget that the privileges of sonship come with responsibilities. Psalm 24:1 says:

"The earth is the Lord's and all it's fulness. The world and those who dwell therein."

The reason for this claim of ownership is clearly stated in verse 2:

"For He has founded it upon the seas. And established it upon the waters."

In other words, it is God's earth because He created it. It does not look like most of the present occupiers of the earth recognise God's ownership. They are making a real mess of it. The sons of God have the responsibility to put things right. Our Father does not only own the things, He owns the people as well. Many do not know this and need to know. Satan pretends his defeat never happened. The sons of God need to bring salvation to the people, salvage the earth and put Satan and his cohorts where they belong, chained in hell.

God Deserves More Sons

Jesus rebukes the Jews thus:

"If God were your Father, you would love Me, for I proceeded forth and came from God; nor have I come of Myself, but He sent Me. Why do you not understand My speech? Because you are not able to listen to My word. You are of your father the devil, and the desires of your father you want to do. He was a murderer from the beginning, and does not stand in the truth, because there is no truth in him. When he speaks a lie, he speaks from his own resources, for he is a liar and the father of it." John 8:43,44

The family tree is very important to the Jews and they pride themselves as descendants of Abraham but in this circumstance, Jesus referred to them as the sons of Satan. This is because they did not behave as Abraham did. Instead their behaviour was like people on assignment for Satan. Their desire to win arguments was blinding them from the truth. They had become liars like Satan. These were people who did not care about the good of others but were completely self-centred. They would lie to promote their own self-interest. When such people are in control politically or socially, there is no progress. The ordinary people suffer and Satan rejoices. **The devil likes to see people suffer. God likes to see people prosper.** It is the responsibility of the sons of God to let all people know this.

One life changing moment for me before I fully committed to the Lord was when I travelled to another African country for work experience, fresh from university. I joined their educational system and was posted to a remote village to help establish a secondary school. The school buildings had been newly built and the teachers' accommodation was okay but the people there were miserable. They practised a form of animist Islam. They attributed all illness and deaths to witchcraft and the Muslim Imam who doubled as witch doctor will usually point out a poor elderly lady as the cause. This woman would be beaten up and branded for life as a witch. Life was wretched for these villagers as this Imam wielded so much power.

I was a nominal Christian then. This means I called myself a Christian and attended church but had not consciously and deliberately invited Jesus into a relationship. **It is important to consciously invite Jesus to be the Lord of your life and prove that you mean it by being totally obedient to Him.** I did this later and saw the difference. Though a nominal Christian, I found the environment very depressing. I set out to do something about the situation. This was no political or economic matter. It was a spiritual matter and I was no expert in spiritual matters. I had to call on God who I barely knew. The handful of students who called themselves Christians seemed completely outnumbered. I invited these ten boys to my house on Sundays to read the psalms, sing songs and say the Lord's prayer. That was all I knew to do and they did not know much either. They all came from one village where a missionary had visited in the past. **Missionaries, lace your boots. There**

is a lost soul somewhere waiting for salvation. God was faithful and did not consider our lack of depth. We turned to him and he turned to us. The thick cloud of heaviness and depression in the atmosphere of the villages changed. The witch hunting reduced. We were invited to village functions. Life returned to the villages. When I left the post after 2 years, we had a bubbling school with volunteer teachers from the UK who promised to continue with my little christian group. I made a pledge to serve the Lord. I recognised the faithfulness and desire of God to respond to us. **God is desperate for sons.**

It is time for the sons of God to stand up and repossess our Father's land as the wrong people, who are in charge, are running things down. We will discuss strategies in later chapters but the first step is to acknowledge your position as a son. Believe in the Lord Jesus Christ, receive Him and become a son.

CHAPTER 5

The Cross is the Heart Of The Matter

"But now in Christ Jesus you who once were far away have been brought near through the blood of Christ. For he himself is our peace, who has made the two one and has destroyed the barrier, the dividing wall of hostility, by abolishing in his flesh the law with its commandments and regulations. His purpose was to create in himself one new man out of the two, thus making peace, and in this one body to reconcile both of them to God through the cross, by which he put to death their hostility." Ephesians 2:13-16

The ultimate purpose of the cross of Jesus Christ is to reconcile man to God. It was a great price to pay but there was no avoiding it. The justice of God demanded the penalty of death for sin.

"For the wages of sin is death, but the gift of God is eternal life in Christ Jesus our Lord" Romans 6:23.

After God had created his beautiful earth and created man in His image. Out of His beautiful earth, He made a beautiful garden for Adam from which blessed man would operate. God gave man the allowance to enjoy everything in the garden except the "tree of sin" (tree of the knowledge of good and evil).

"for in the day that you eat of it you shall surely die." (Genesis 2:17).

In spite of God's warning and the abundance of trees available to Adam and Eve, they disobeyed God and were therefore cut off from God, plunging the rest of mankind into the darkness of the absence of God. Humanity descended from Adam and Eve so if the two lived in darkness, the rest of humanity would live in darkness. Humanity groped around in darkness. There was no pathway to lead us to light. We were condemned to accidents, especially in an environment unknown to us.

Except someone brings light into your darkness to lead you out of it, you are condemned to ignorance and destruction.

"My people are destroyed for lack of knowledge" (Hosea 4:6).

There are people who go around pretending to have the knowledge to lead people to the light. Many times, you only have to take one look at them and know that these so called gurus, masters or prophets need some light themselves. Jesus calls them 'the blind leading the blind.' Many desperate gropers fall for their lies.

There is only one 'Light of the world' and that is Jesus Christ.

"Then Jesus spoke to them again, saying, "I am the light of the world. He who follows Me shall not walk in darkness, but have the light of life."(John 8:12).

A few years ago, as I sat behind my desk in the office, God gave me an open vision. An open vision is when God changes the scene right before your open eyes to convey a message to you. I looked out and saw the terrace buildings crumbling unto the street. Yet down below, a great number of people were going about their business ignoring the crumbling buildings and the bricks that were just about to crush them. The scene change before my eyes into the Prime Minister's office where I saw the cabinet overwhelmed and confused not knowing what to do about the calamitous situation. The Lord showed me a small number amongst the people on the street who seemed to be lit up. He spoke into my spirit that the answer to the problems of our nations are in the hands of the sons of light.

The interpretation to this vision is simply that the answer to the woes of this world lies in Jesus Christ and His brethren whom He has appointed as the sons of light. *"You are the light of the world." (Matthew 5:14).*

What Is the Light of God?

The light of God is God's glory. God's glory is all that He is: His truth, wisdom, power, majesty; His essential nature. This is what he planned for man when he created man in his own image and likeness; that man would be everything he God is. He is light and therefore man would be light. The presence of God is what ignites that light. The absence of God plunges you into darkness. **Spiritual death is the loss of the light of God.** When God comes in, he comes with his light. When he goes out, he goes with his light. When he comes with his light, things turn the right way up.

Wherever our team goes to minister. We are confident of bringing the light of God into the place. The light of God is his glory. His glory includes his power of healing and deliverance. Because we have allowed him to come and live inside of us, we carry his light around. As long as you do not block his glory with unbelief and sin, expect the glory of God to manifest. **Expect God's power when you step out in His name.** This is possible because of the price Jesus paid on the Cross of Calvary.

The cradle of our ministry is a place called Harlesden in the north western part of London, UK. The area of Harlesden & Stonebridge were notorious for crime in the 1990s. The neglected

Council built estates and the proliferation of drugs and police 'no go' areas meant that the darkest ruled the day. Anyone who could afford it moved out of the area. There were several empty Council flats on Stonebridge estates because even the homeless did not want to live there. At this time, there were so many deaths on the streets of Harlesden and Stonebridge that one newspaper referred to the area as the murder capital of Europe. This is where God placed us. You would invite people to church and they would tell you to the face they could not come because of our unsafe location. It was difficult to find insurers for our equipment. Yet we had the assurance that when light shines in the darkness, the darkness must disappear. We had become partakers of the light of God through the price paid on the Cross at Calvary. We partnered with other Christian ministries in prayer and social outreaches. Today light has replaced darkness in Harlesden and Stonebridge. The infamous Stonebridge Estate has been replaced by a brand new building project with all the modern amenities; new churches have sprung up; many former residents are coming back; crime figures have fallen dramatically. The police station which was upgraded in the nineties has been down graded to an outpost. It is a well sought after area in terms of accommodation and social life. All this achieved by the light of God. In later chapters, I will give you specific incidents and strategies that led to this change. There is still more work to be done in the area but Stonebridge is smiling again and hope has replaced despair. It takes the sons of God to bring change to the land.

Light In His Soul

When the man of God invited me to visit him in South Africa and see his work amongst the Shangaani people in the Limpopo area, I was excited. He had planted many churches in the remote but beautiful villages in this region. I met this saintly man at the centenary celebration of the Azusa Street Revival in Los Angeles. We liked each other and became friends. I do a lot of city ministry but rural ministry draws me like a magnet. It was a long eleven hour flight to Johannesburg from London Heathrow and a further 7 hour journey by car to this lovely part of South Africa. The hospitality of my hosts was amazing. When we sat down for breakfast, the first morning, unbeknown to me, I was talking about things going on in the village that I could possibly not have known about. I was giving such accurate words of knowledge about the village. 'Word of knowledge' is when God speaks things through you about events that you could not possibly and naturally know about except by the revelation of God. This is a supernatural manifestation of the light of God. My hosts were so baffled that they went to invite the village chief to come and listen to me.

The village chief was in his own darkness. Though a Christian, he had seen his wife die in a horrible accident a few months earlier. This had plunged him into a deep depression. He had not prayed to God or been to any church service since then. **Depression is the absence of hope. The absence of hope is the absence of light. The absence of light means the absence of God.** I could see the heaviness and darkness on the chief's spirit begin to lift as he listened to me.

Laughter was beginning to replace self-pity. I invited him to my first meeting. He came and was seated in the congregation. During the service, he stood up and danced to the front praising God. The darkness had lifted. The place erupted with joy as they saw their depressed chief come back to life. The light of God had gone into his soul and dispelled all darkness. My reward was that I received a personal tour of many historical sites with this veteran freedom fighter as my guide. We had many laughs together before I left South Africa. **Light will always triumph over darkness.**

Do you have the light of God In You?

The light of God is attractive. When God is at home in you, people see it. This is not to say you will have no detractors. Even those who oppose you will notice the glory.

"You are the light of the world. A city on a hill cannot be hidden. Neither do people light a lamp and put it under a bowl. Instead they put it on its stand, and it gives light to everyone in the house. In the same way, let your light shine

before men, that they may see your good deeds and praise your Father in heaven." Matthew 5:14-16

There are many who call themselves Christians but are not manifesting the light of God. It is the Spirit of God in you that gives you the right to call yourself a Christian. **You must be born again by the Spirit of God.** You could preach the gospel but if there is no light of God coming out of you to back it, it is ineffective. I have spoken to many who have cited the behaviour of some Christians as the reason why they oppose Christianity. I am not holding brief for the many excuses people give to continue wallowing in their darkness. The people of the world recognise the light of God, so if you call yourself a Christian and you do not manifest the glory, they will point it out to you. Jesus said,

"The prince of this world comes and he has nothing in me." (John 14:30)

When Jesus was put before the High Priests and the Roman governor, Pontius Pilate, they found it difficult to manufacture lies against Him. They could only accuse Him with the truth He had spoken. They called it blasphemy. Yet before his death, many of these same accusers followed him wherever he went because they enjoyed his light. Jesus says of John:

"John was a lamp that burned and gave light, and you chose for a time to enjoy his light." John 5:35 (NIV)

The light of God has been given to you to be enjoyed by others. How many are enjoying your light? Your family, your friends, your community and the world have to enjoy your light. Freely you have received, freely give.

Your Debt is Paid in Full

Man's disobedience in the garden of Eden kicked God out of Adams life. He had broken God's law and was therefore guilty. The supreme court of heaven pronounced a judgement of "guilty" on Adam. He was sentenced to a life without God; life in darkness. He owed a debt he could not pay. God's unmerited favour and deep love kicked into play. A plan to rescue Adam was set in motion. Heaven's law cannot be over-ruled.

Adam's debt had to be cleared. As Adam himself was not capable of paying it, someone else had to come to his rescue. Jesus came to the rescue. He paid the debt he did not owe. Man owed a debt he could not pay. Love came to the rescue.

The original intention for the creation of man by God was to share with man all that is His (God's). He would therefore not allow the weakness of man to jeopardise this plan. His strength would step in for man.

"But God demonstrates his own love for us in this: While we were still sinners, Christ died for us.

Since we have now been justified by his blood, how much more shall we be saved from God's wrath through him! For if, when we were God's enemies, we were reconciled to him through the death of his Son, how much more, having been reconciled, shall we be saved through his life! Not only is this so, but we also rejoice in God through our Lord Jesus Christ, through whom we have now received reconciliation." Romans 5:8-11

By going through the most horrible death anyone could face at that time, that is, death on the cross, Jesus paid the full price for the sins of mankind. Isaiah prophesied it:

*"But He was wounded for our transgressions,
He was bruised for our iniquities;
The chastisement for our peace was upon Him,
And by His stripes we are healed.
All we like sheep have gone astray;
We have turned, every one, to his own way;
And the Lord has laid on Him the iniquity of us all."
(Isaiah 53:5-6)*

Paul understood it:

"There is therefore now no condemnation to those who are in Christ Jesus, who do not walk according to the flesh, but according to the Spirit. For the law of the Spirit of life in Christ Jesus has made me free from the law of sin and death." (Romans 8:1-2)

We must embrace the truth that the price for our sins has been paid. We should therefore reject the accusations of the enemy, a strategy he uses to weaken our hands so he can manipulate us.

Without the Cross of Jesus Christ, there is no freedom and therefore no good news to tell the world. The crucifixion and resurrection of Jesus

Christ and the consequence of it is our message as Christians. Any other message has to have this at the core, otherwise there is no resurrection power to back your word. The power is in the Cross. When the Cross is preached, it hits the depths of your soul. Paul says in 1 Corinthians 1:18:

"For the message of the Cross is foolishness unto those who are perishing but to us who are being saved, it is the power of God.

CHAPTER 6

The Blood Of Jesus

It is difficult to be indifferent about any blood. You may shriek at the sight of it or remain calm but there is something in blood that screams "life". In the Old Testament, in the days of the daily sacrifice of animals to God, the tabernacle would have been a very bloody place. I can also imagine how blood everywhere would have reminded the priests, levites and the Israelites the number of sacrifices needed to appease our God. They had to sacrifice animals everyday. The special sacrifice of the Day of Atonement had to be repeated every year.

The day of Atonement was one day in the year when special sacrifices are made for the sins of all of Israel. It was the only day when a national fast was mandatory. It was also the only day when the High Priest could enter the

Holy of Holies (the inner chamber where God had promised His presence would dwell). This exercise had to be repeated every year, when blood was brought to the Mercy Seat of the Holy of Holies.

The blood of Abel cried out for vengeance in Genesis 4:10. Jesus, in a rebuke of the Pharisees and other detractors in Luke 11:50 warns that the blood of all the prophets Israel had killed was on that generation and was crying out for vengeance:

"That the blood of all the prophets which was shed from the foundation of the world may be required of this generation, from the blood of Abel to the blood of Zechariah who perished between the altar and the temple. Yes, I say to you, it shall be required of this generation." (Luke 11:50-51)

The Blood of Jesus cries out "Mercy". His is the blood of love. Pure love. God is light. In him is no darkness at all. It is impossible for the Blood of Jesus to cry out anything but mercy. While he yet hung on the cross and His killers were taunting Him, He prayed: " Father forgive them for they do not know what they are doing." Mercy cries out for all who need mercy. Are you overwhelmed with the guilt and condemnation of sin? The Blood Of Jesus is crying out for you:

Therefore, brethren, having boldness to enter the Holiest by the blood of Jesus, by a new and living way which He consecrated for us, through the veil, that is, His flesh, and having a High Priest over the house of God, let us draw near with a true heart in full assurance of faith, having our hearts sprinkled from an evil conscience and our bodies washed with pure water. (Hebrews 10:19-22).

The Blood Of Jesus cleanses us from all sin. It washes your conscience and makes it white as snow. To acknowledge one's sinfulness and throw ourselves on the mercy of God is an experience everyone needs to have. It is the best experience anyone could have. God has made it available to everyone. All must know about this.

It happened to me in a hospital bed. I had been in an accident and the bones in my left leg were crushed. I had been lying on my back for a couple of months waiting for some infections to subside so the surgeons could proceed with a bone graft. The prognosis was dim. My soul was in a dark depression. A young lady who regularly came to visit her dad in the same ward had this enviable cheerfulness about her. There was light shining from deep within her, a quiet confidence. She would often pass by my bed and speak to me about the delivering power of the Cross of Jesus Christ. I fancied myself as a Christian and would often concur to what she said without giving much thought to it. One day, at my lowest emotionally and having nowhere to turn, I remembered "mercy". I pulled my covering sheets over my head, acknowledged my sins, confessed my faith in the finished work of the Cross of Jesus Christ and asked Jesus to come and live in me and become the Lord of my life. Hope replaced despair and faith replaced fear. A miracle had happened in my heart.

I had done many things in the past in the Name of Jesus and seen some results. I had led 'Christian' groups and was church going. I had enjoyed the peace and emotion at church services but this feeling was different. It was as if my conscience had been scraped of every grain of guilt and anxiety and truck loads of hope had been poured in my spirit. **The Blood of Jesus brings**

forgiveness, cleansing and justification. This experience transformed me to the extent that when the team of doctors came round my bed that day, I countered their gloomy assessment with "I will walk again and be out of here in no time because of Jesus." They were dismissive of my prophecy but quite happy that I was uncharacteristically full of cheer. Well, my prophecy came to pass and a few short weeks I was out of the hospital completely healed and desperate for more of Jesus. I know there are many who have had similar experiences, some more dramatic, others less so. The difference is the Blood of Jesus.

The Blood of Jesus is an ever flowing blood shouting mercy to all who will listen. Remind yourself and confess with your mouth what the Blood of Jesus has done for you. It frightens Satan every time you mention the Blood of Jesus. Satan and his cohorts know the power of the blood and will flee. We have special meetings at our church, Joy House, during the feast of Crucifixion and Resurrection. We dedicate this as a special festival to the Cross and the Blood. Apart from the many salvations we see, we have come to expert remarkable miracles, especially blood miracles. We have seen many blood disorders corrected; abnormal flow of blood cease. A lady who was anxious about a growth in the anal area had her miracle by the Blood. She came praising the Lord that the sizeable growth had disappeared.

Sweet Covenant

How would you feel if you had the richest person in the world come to you and tell you I am taking over all your debts and you can have free access to all my possessions if you would agree to marry me? Now this person is not only the richest but also the most beautiful, the kindest, gentlest, the most peaceful; the best in all good things. I am sure this would be a proposal hard to refuse. The good news is, all of us have such a proposal freely placed before us not by the richest or best in this world but by the creator and master of the universe.

Jesus Christ has sworn by blood to fulfil every promise he has made in his word to us.

We need to understand that God's relationship with us is based on unchangeable covenant from an unchanging God. He has put His offer on the table. If you want to be part of this covenant, you will have to accept the terms of the covenant, put your signature to it and not quit. In the world we live in, we are bound to enter several agreements. We are always advised to read the small print of every document before we sign. This is because deceivers who want to take advantage of you do not want you to see the unfavourable parts of the agreement. They therefore put this in small print. **You can trust God. He has emptied Himself. Every part of Him is in bold capitals. The Cross is His message.**

Greater love has no one than this, than to lay down one's life for his friends. (John 15:13)

It stands to reason that if I can give up my life for you then there is nothing I will keep from you. Jesus was not suicidal, neither was he a pretender wanting to prove a point. He manifested the glory of the Father, full of grace and truth. He healed the sick, raised the dead and performed outstanding miracles. **The sacrifice of Jesus on the Cross was a voluntary act of love.** Love is all he is and he has put this on the table. Your part is to receive this love. Sign on to this agreement by offering to live for Him. Make your life his so his life can become yours. I woke up one morning singing a song with the following lyrics:

Your blood is mine; my blood is yours
I thank you Jesus for the Cross.
My life is yours; Your life is mine
I thank you Jesus for the Cross

O the Blood, Sweet sweet Blood
I thank you Jesus for the Cross

This song sums up covenant. We sing it in church especially during the Lord's Supper and it lifts us.

Covenant is a marriage where the two become one flesh. God has given special power in His word to the agreement of two or three. There shall be no conclusion to a matter until there are two or three witnesses (Deuteronomy 19:15). Jesus promised in Matthew 18: 19-20 that when two agree as concerning anything on earth it will be done for them in Heaven. He also promises to be present where two or three are gathered together in His Name. The key word in all these examples is agreement. The eighteenth chapter of Matthew deals with humility, forgiveness, reconciliation and sacrifice in order to come to the place of agreement and power.

God is obedient to His own Word because He is one with His Word.

For there are three that bear witness in heaven: the Father, the Word, and the Holy Spirit; and these three are one. And there are three that bear witness on earth: the Spirit, the water, and the blood; and these three agree as one. (1 John 5:7-8).

For you to establish that God is indeed present, you need three witnesses: The love of the Father, the truth of the Word (Son) and the power of the Holy Spirit. Do not settle for just one or two of them. All three must be present. Every church assembly must ensure these three, which are one, is present. We should continually pray "your kingdom come and Your will be done on earth as it is in heaven."

For us on earth to establish we are sound and completely in covenant, we also need three witnesses: The guidance and provision of the Holy Spirit, repentance signified by the waters of baptism as well as a continuous attitude of repentance and righteousness occasioned by the Blood of Jesus Christ. Some have zeroed in on the one or other but there is the need to have all three because out of the mouth of two or three witnesses a matter shall be established.

This quotation from Genesis 2:24-25 sums up covenant beautifully:

"Therefore a man shall leave his father and mother and be joined to his wife, and they shall become one flesh. And they were both naked, the man and his wife, and were not ashamed."

CHAPTER 7

The Breath of God

The restoration of God's breath is a return of God's presence and mandate as at the beginning in the Garden of Eden. Adam and eve could not fulfil God's plan for their lives because they lost the breath of God. God's assignment to them was to be fruitful, multiply, fill the earth, subdue it and have dominion.

The Breath of God is the Holy Spirit. The Holy Spirit is the Spirit of God; the power of God. He is God. To acknowledge Him and talk about him is by itself a translation to a different dimension of God's presence. Every time we have acknowledged the presence of the Holy Spirit and spoken about Him, He has shown Himself tangibly. **The Breath of God makes the difference.** When God gives an assignment to any one, He has to give the equipment to accomplish this assignment. God cannot equip with anything inferior to Himself. He anoints you with Himself. **When God appoints, He anoints. All God given assignments must be accomplished with the power of the Holy Spirit otherwise will fall short of expectation.** The Holy Spirit is not acknowledged enough among Christians. Some 'Christians' do not acknowledge Him at all. Yet there is no Christianity without the Holy Spirit. The Christian church was birthed in Acts chapter 2 when the Holy Spirit filled the room and the people where the disciples were gathered. You cannot be born again or call yourself the son of God without the Holy Spirit.

In the Garden of Eden, what Adam and Eve lost when they were deceived by the devil was the Holy Spirit, the Breath of God. For anyone to be born again into the category of a son, you need to receive the Holy Spirit. Why did Adam & Eve lose the Holy Spirit? The Holy Spirit is God; He is a person; He is holy. **The Holy Spirit cannot dwell where there is sin.**

Ezekiel saw the departure of God's glory from the temple in Ezekiel 10. This is an indication that there was so much sin that the glory of God could not continue to abide in the temple where he had promised that His name would dwell. **The Glory of God is the physical manifestation of the Holy Spirit.** You cannot move in disobedience to God and expect the Spirit of God to be there with you. I have cautioned several people who feel they have the right to continue in anger because they have been wronged. Unforgiving or angry spirit are 'no go' areas to the Holy Spirit. There are many who have lost the presence of the Holy Spirit because of an unforgiving spirit. Jesus says in *Matthew 5:23,24* that before you bring your gift on the altar go and reconcile with your brother first.

Unforgiveness Can Be Costly

This cheerful Christian lady who loved the Lord and was a minister in her church could not find a satisfying employment for a long time. When she did, she could not hold it down for more than a few weeks. I became concerned as it was affecting her self-esteem. I went to the Lord about it and the Holy Spirit revealed to me the need for her to be reconciled to her mother. I invited her to my office and in conversation, mentioned her Mum. This pretty lady suddenly contorted with rage in front of me. She was swearing on top of her voice about all the wrongs she had suffered at the hands of her Mum. I listened to her, quietly praying for the healing of her soul. After a few minutes of ranting and raving, she broke down in tears. I had great compassion for her. I reminded her of the 5th commandment:

"Honour your father and mother that it may be well with you and your days will be long on the land which the Lord your God is giving you."

She left my office still unsure about what to do. The good news is, when she came by my office a few months later. She was bubbly. She had made up with her Mum and spent Christmas with her. She now had a job she enjoyed and had held on to it. She was grateful for the godly counsel. Her Mum passed on a few months later and left her a good inheritance. Forgive and see blessings that have been locked up released to you. We have seen many healed physically as they forgave.

"Blessed are the peacemakers for they shall be called the sons of God." Matthew 5:9

The Holy Spirit Is God

The Holy Spirit is not wind but He moves like wind; the Holy Spirit is not a bird but sometimes He comes in gently as a dove; the Holy Spirit is not fire though when He comes, He can burn like fire. He is not a force or a magnetic field. The Holy Spirit is God, the third person of the Trinity with specific responsibilities especially for the sons of God. Our senior brother, Jesus, needed Him for the wisdom of God, for performance of miracles, to comfort Him and to raise Him from the dead. We also need Him.

"The Spirit of the Lord is upon Me,
Because He has anointed Me
To preach the gospel to the poor;
He has sent Me to heal the brokenhearted,
To proclaim liberty to the captives

*And recovery of sight to the blind,
To set at liberty those who are oppressed;
To proclaim the acceptable year of the Lord." Luke 4:18,19*

The assignment of the Holy Spirit

The first assignment of the Holy Spirit is to get us born again. The starting point for any human being for a life that makes sense is to be born again. From the time of our separation from God through disobedience in the Garden of Eden, man has been groping in the dark. We do not understand ourselves or the purpose of our existence. We suddenly discover that we exist and get into survival mode. We need to survive. We get into a defensive war. The fear of death hangs over us. As we make our slow progress towards inevitable death, we seek to make life as comfortable as we can. Hopefully if we are able to get physical comfort, it might just take away some of the anxieties in life. Man is therefore pre-occupied with possessing things. We strive to make as much money as we can because money can buy things and give us influence. It is an empty life without the breath of God. It is a lonely life of rejection if heaven does not partner with us and reveal the purpose for our creation. It is like being dumped on a strange island with no idea of how you got there and striving to live because death is a more fearful prospect.

This is what moved Nicodemus, a well to do and respected community leader to approach Jesus. He had observed Jesus move with an understanding, confidence and authority that was beyond normal human ability. He had observed Jesus operate by the power of the Holy Spirit. He approaches Jesus and acknowledges his perception of the power of God in His life. Jesus immediately reveals what makes the difference. For you to experience the kingdom of God which is what Nicodemus observed operating in Jesus, one must be born again. This language confuses Nicodemus. The response of Jesus Christ is:

"Most assuredly, I say to you, unless one is born of water and the Spirit, he cannot enter the kingdom of God. That which is born of the flesh is flesh, and that which is born of the Spirit is spirit. Do not marvel that I said to you, 'You must be born again.' The wind blows where it wishes, and

you hear the sound of it, but cannot tell where it comes from and where it goes. So is everyone who is born of the Spirit."(John 3:5-8)

The secret of eternal life is to be born by the spirit of God. Jesus reveals in John 3:16 that the Love of God has made eternal life available to us through Jesus Christ. God's purpose for mankind is not to judge or condemn man but to save. He offers us a brand new life; a new life as if our former life never happened. This life is in union with God through the power of the Holy Spirit. **Every man needs to be born again.**

I have met people who have told me they are Christian only to stutter when it comes to the question of whether they are born again. We need to be born again so we can have a special relationship with God. God is spirit and they that worship him must worship him in spirit and truth. It is impossible to experience true spiritual worship if you are not born again.

I was recently invited to lead a group of people including government officials in prayer. My opening statement was "every one needs to meet with Jesus and be born again." An uncomfortable quietness descended on the place because there were officials there from other religions and this was supposed to be a formal meeting and no one was supposed to cause offence. I did not intend to cause offence. I had good news on my heart that I could not keep. After I had explained that I was a nominal Christian who did not know any better till I met with Jesus, the atmosphere relaxed a bit. It was clear that Jesus was above all our religions and is available to all Muslims, Hindus, Sikhs, Christians, Atheists, Humanists and Witches. As many as would call on Him. I had the opportunity to lay hands on an official who belonged to one of the religions. The gentleman held on tightly to me wanting what I had. He went home a liberated man, set free by the power of the Holy Spirit although with his turban still in place.

The second assignment of the Holy Spirit is to be our Helper. Not only does he get us born again, He stays with us to babysit us and guide us through our life as the sons of God. The Greek word translated Helper could also be translated Comforter or Advocate. Jesus told His disciples that if they believed in Him, they would do the works that He had done and even greater works. How were they going to do that? He explained in the next few verses, John 14:15-17:

"If you love Me, keep My commandments. And I will pray the Father, and He will give you another Helper, that He may abide with you forever— the Spirit of truth, whom the world cannot receive, because it neither sees Him nor knows Him; but you know Him, for He dwells with you and will be in you.

The Holy Spirit has been given to us as a personal assistant. This is no ordinary assistant. He is an assistant who knows infinitely better than we do. He will prompt us at every turn but will not violate our will. It is wise to consult Him before any decision is made. In the Old Testament of the Bible, the kings who excelled were those who sought the counsel of God before any assignment. As born again sons of God, the Holy Spirit is not only walking closely by our side, He has also come to live inside of us. Let us not ignore such a wonderful privilege.

I try to be constantly aware of the presence of the Holy Spirit with me and seek His direction before I make any move. I need to know how He wants me to minister. If I don't hear His voice, I feel lonely. I have come to realise that if I am not hearing Him, it is not His fault, it is mine. I need to separate myself in prayer and where necessary, fasting. A life of prayer is key to life in the Spirit. When he directs, there is contentment for everyone.

I was on a three-city preaching tour. The Holy Spirit would give me what he wanted me to say and do at each service in each city. I prepared well before the day but He always surprised me with wonderful insights even as I ministered. Every preacher who acknowledges the Holy Spirit would agree with this fact. It is however the most uncomfortable thing when you leave home blank. It does happen some times though. I have realised that on such occasions the ministry of the Holy Spirit is extraordinary in spite of my discomfort. Though I never seem to get used to it. I was arriving in the third city of my tour and was due to preach in a large church. The people did not know me and the carnal me wanted to make a good impression but I had no message. In my desperate bid to hear from God, I had unwittingly shut my spiritual ears. My Helper was at hand. Just before we hit the church auditorium, He opened my eyes and gave me an open vision. Though I was wide awake, the natural scenery had blocked off and He showed me three scenes playing before me as in a movie. As I got to the auditorium, He gave me utterance and I spoke on those three things. The whole auditorium erupted with amazement, especially the pastors and leaders. They were on their feet through my ministry time. God had given them a prophetic word concerning those three things and I had brought confirmation. This was a major direction move for the church.

The Holy Spirit is our Comforter. Psalm 34:19 tells us that the affliction of the righteous are many but the Lord God delivers him from them all. Being born again and having the Holy Spirit with you does not exempt you from moments when you need the comforting arms of the Holy Spirit around you. Jesus would have benefited from the comforting arms of the Holy Spirit when He heard Herod had beheaded John the Baptist.

When Jesus wept over Jerusalem, the Holy Spirit would have been there to comfort Him. I have sat with many a family who but for the comforting arm of the Holy Spirit would have been inconsolable. Everyone who has walked with the Holy Spirit has a testimony of the comforting arm of the Holy Spirit. When I came out of a meeting with one of my leaders who was offended and leaving the church, I was perplexed. This congregant had used very cruel words and made me look heartless. I felt sorrowful. As soon as I stepped out I had a text message from an unlikely source. The message simply read, "You have a Father's heart." I knew this was the Holy Spirit. I was immediately comforted. In my heaviness of heart, I had forgotten the Comforter was as close to me as the breath in my nostrils. I would not acknowledge Him in my self-pity. He therefore had to comfort me from afar through the text message.

The Holy Spirit is our advocate. He speaks for us. In Acts 1:8, Jesus tells His disciples they shall receive power after the Holy Spirit had come upon them and they shall be His witness. They could not be proper witnesses without the baptism of the Holy Spirit. The Holy Spirit would be the evidence of their message. He will speak for them. In John 10:38 Jesus admonishes His hearers that if they do not believe in him, they should believe in the works He is doing. In other words, they should not ignore the advocacy of the Holy Spirit. The Holy Spirit is our most loyal cheer leader if we would allow Him. **The Holy Spirit changes us from the inside.** He transforms us to be salt and light of the world. He changes ugly people into beautiful saints.

The third assignment of the Holy Spirit is to empower us with supernatural ability.

But you shall receive power when the Holy Spirit has come upon you; and you shall be witnesses to Me in Jerusalem, and in all Judea and Samaria, and to the end of the earth." (Acts 1:8)

The power spoken about here is not just the power of utterance but also the ability to perform miracles, signs and wonders. The gospel of Jesus Christ is accompanied by supernatural manifestations. Miracles are amazing supernatural happenings that are beyond human ability. We expect miracles at our meetings because they are Holy Spirit meetings and we often see miracles. Holy Spirit filled people should always expect miracles in their lives. Those who know the heart of God and acknowledge the power of the Holy Spirit are witnesses to a miracle working God. The miracles of God are to repair damages and bring fuller lives. There is a purpose to God's miracles: To reveal Jesus Christ and draw people to the kingdom of God. Psychic power and supernatural manifestation of the ungodly kind do not produce fruit beneficial for enhancement of life.

A few years ago people were falling over each other to see a calf idol drinking milk at a religious temple in London. It was reported in the national newspapers. Another guy made a fortune by bending spoons through psychic means. Some are able to tell you things they could not possibly have known in the natural, through the occult. If the supernatural activity is not bringing life and pointing to Jesus, ignore it. We thank God that the Holy Spirit is mending lives all over the world even if the national papers would not report them. Eventually they will, because truth shall prevail. For us who believe in the available miracle working power of the Holy Spirit, there is nothing more rewarding than the gratitude you see on the face of a mended life. The Holy Spirit is willing to restore. I can still see the face of that young South African boy whose heartbeat was so loud and so fast that his face displayed fear of death, but as soon as hands were laid on him, he was delivered from this birth condition and exploded into uncontrollable joy. He is now a healthy young man grateful to Jesus Christ for what the Holy Spirit did in his life.

Another young man did not know Jesus and had only come to one of our meetings at the University of Ghana as a videographer. God had other plans. His career as a talented national footballer had been cut short by a serious back injury. The Holy Spirit intervened at the meeting and healed him. He also gave his life to the Lord. He started football training again that same week. We have seen the Holy Spirit do several miracles for which we give God all the glory. The Holy Spirit is in the miracle business. All over the world, blind eyes are being open, the lame are walking, the dead raised, financial and other miracles are displaying the power of the Holy Spirit.

This power is available to every believer, not just pulpit ministers, as a witness unto Jesus. Everyone who receives Jesus as Lord receives the wisdom and power of God in the form of the Holy Spirit.

"For Jews request a sign, and Greeks seek after wisdom; but we preach Christ crucified, to the Jews a stumbling block and to the Greeks foolishness, but to those who are called, both Jews and Greeks, Christ the power of God and the wisdom of God. Because the foolishness of God is wiser than men, and the weakness of God is stronger than men." (1 Corinthians 1:22-25)

The Holy Spirit will overwhelm the senses of your listeners with His power. They will see miracles, they will hear wisdom, they will taste of the goodness of God, they will smell the fragrance of life and they will feel the power of His touch.

CHAPTER 8

The Real You

Let the sons of God stand up. Are you real or fake? Friend, if you have believed in the sacrifice of the cross of Jesus Christ and accepted the finished work of the Blood of Jesus Christ and received Him as your Lord and brother, you are a real son of God. You better stand up and let His glory shine through you.

"He was in the world, and the world was made through Him, and the world did not know Him. He came to His own, and His own did not receive Him. But as many as received Him, to them He gave the right to become children of God, to those who believe in His name: who were born, not of blood, nor of the will of the flesh, nor of the will of man, but of God." (John 1:10-13)

What is fake is the life we lived when we walked around without God and without hope. We were manipulated by Satan and his cohorts to live a defeated life. Satan hates God and hates you. Satan is all darkness and no light. There is no love in Satan. As one can only give what they have, Satan is incapable of doing good because he has no good in him. When we walk under his authority, we are manipulated to live a life that is not original to us. A life that we can only describe as fake. I can only imagine the heartbreak of God as He observes us, created in His image and likeness, deceived into fruitless existence. Man was vulnerable before the intervention of Jesus. Satan therefore bullied man. God did something about the predicament of man. The Cross of Jesus Christ paved the way for man to be reconciled to God and become acquainted with his real self and destiny. The righteousness we receive by our faith in the Cross of Jesus Christ empowers us to live as sons of God, no less.

Righteousness simply means we are back to our original position next to God. No sin divides us from God. Where we were guilty and therefore not fit to stand before God, we have been declared "innocent". Jesus has paid the price for our guilt. The power of Satan over our lives is broken. He no longer has the power to manipulate us. God has got His sons back. **It is heartbreaking for God to see His sons, for whom He has paid the ultimate price, continue to behave like slaves of Satan.**

How sons of God live

Sons of God live like God. Every good father would want his children to have the best quality of life. Many of us humans desire our children to have a better quality of life than we have had. This is an admission that we fall short of perfection. We desire that, if possible, our children would have perfect lives. Well, God is perfect and what He desires is that His children would live like Him.

The entrance to God's presence is the Blood of Jesus Christ. There is no other way. Jesus said in John 14:6:

"I am the way, the truth and the life. No one comes to the Father except through me."

There is no other way to God except through the Blood of Jesus Christ. When you come through the Blood, you are home and free. One common character of little children is the confidence they have in their parents. Until the parents give them reason not to believe in them, kids will swallow every promise you give to them and will remind you of it if you fail to fulfil. You can trust God. He will not give you a promise he cannot fulfil. He created the heavens and the earth and all things in it.

Your first assignment as a son of God is to make a decision to ground yourself in faith.

"But without faith it is impossible to please Him, for he who comes to God must believe that He is, and that He is a rewarder of those who diligently seek Him."(Hebrews 11:6)

If you have come home to God as a son then stay at home. Your life as a wanderer has come to an end. You are no longer a vagabond. The presence of the Holy Spirit brings an assurance that produces hope. This hope will not fail because it is anchored in the sure Word of God. Before you made this decision to come home, you were a wanderer. You were all over the place seeking peace for your soul. Peace is satisfaction and contentment. As unlikely as it may sound, our revelry, debauchery, thieving and all addictions are the result of our search for peace. The irony of it is that it draws us deeper into confusion.

God is stable and fixed. Being rooted and having confidence are what God is. He is the beginning and the end. Jesus told His listeners that He knew where He was coming from and where He was going. He was therefore confident. He had a straight path to walk. Making a decision for Jesus would lose you some friends and possessions because those things fall outside your chosen path.

I gave the good news of Jesus Christ to a man who was steeped in another religious practice. He received Jesus into his life and enjoyed the Christian faith yet he was not ready to change his lifestyle or get rid of some of the symbols associated with the old religion. **When you get into a new covenant with Jesus Christ, all old covenants and its symbols must leave your**

life. My friend and new found brother refused to do this. He did not do a complete turn around. It was not long before he slipped back into his old lifestyle of excesses. Jesus asked his would-be disciples to deny themselves, pick up their cross and follow Him. If you give the devil a lift, he would end up driving the car.

Faith is unyielding confidence in God. In your walk with God, who is now your father, every challenge in life is a test of your faith. Are you going to believe that, contrary to His word, your heavenly father would forsake you? I want to assure you that it is impossible for God to forsake you. You need this assurance yourself. You can only get this by receiving and keeping the word of God in your heart.

The grace of God has given us the Bible, the gift of His written word. All that He is and all He would be, He has given to us in His written word. Make it your companion. Read the Word and believe it. Ignore the argument of detractors that the Bible was written by men and therefore are the thoughts of man.

"All Scripture is given by inspiration of God, and is profitable for doctrine, for reproof, for correction, for instruction in righteousness, that the man of God may be complete, thoroughly equipped for every good work." (2 Timothy 3:16)

Although men wrote what is in the Bible, they were inspired by God. That is how God uses man. If you would make yourself available as an obedient son, God would do things through you as if He was doing it Himself. Jesus told Philip *"When you see Me you have seen the Father"*. Do not be distracted from the daily reading of the word of God.

As a son you are not only limited to the written word. Every father wants to speak to his son. You also have the privilege of the spoken word. The Father will not violate His own law of witness. He therefore wants to confirm His written word by speaking it to your spirit. Faith and assurance come when his written word is confirmed in your spirit by His spoken word. You will hear your Father speak when you still your spirit in prayer before Him.

"Be still, and know that I am God"(Psalm 46:10).

One of the most effective ways I have found in stilling my spirit is praying in other tongues. This prayer language builds your spirit up in the battle against a truant soul. When you pray in other tongues you build your spirit up (1 Corinthians 14:4). It is important that you speak in other tongues because you speak to God. The Message Bible puts it this way:

"If you praise him in the private language of tongues, God understands you but no one else does, for you are sharing intimacies just between you and him." (1 Corinthians 14:2)

Just like a parent may understand the "I am hungry", "I am wet", "I want to be picked up" noises of their little baby, God understands every word that comes out of our mouth. He interprets it by our hearts. He uses that communication channel to speak to us himself. He speaks through us in tongues and we have to interpret it to build the church. When I pray in tongues, my spirit becomes sharp and sensitive to the voice and prompting of God. **God's voice builds faith.**

The Son Lives in Obedience

Jesus says in John 5:30 that His judgement is right because He judges according to what He hears from the Father. The rest of that chapter talks about how the Father has entrusted Him with immense power because of His obedience. In the father and son covenant we have with God through Jesus Christ, our part is to obey. The Father's part is to lead, protect and provide. **When we do not obey, we are out of covenant and have no right to expect covenant fruit.** Obedience is to execute His will. His will is clearly expressed in Ephesians 1:9,10:

"having made known to us the mystery of His will, according to His good pleasure which He purposed in Himself, that in the dispensation of the fullness of the times He might gather together in one all things in Christ, both which are in heaven and which are on earth—in Him."

The will of the Father is to gather all things in heaven and earth in Christ. It is clear that our assignment, as earth residents is to ensure that all things on earth are gathered in Christ. What are the things on earth? The people and the land.

The land includes the animals and all the others that live on the land. Our life ambition as sons is to ensure that all the people and all the land are gathered in Christ Jesus. We know this will surely happen. God has promised it.

"Truly, as I live, all the earth shall be filled with the glory of the Lord" (Numbers 14:21).

Some people will use the gift of their free will to decide not to come back home to God. Many others will come back to God. Everyone who responds to this call of the Father through His Son will be saved and given new life. The question is whether we are going to be obedient sons who will be obedient to the Father's will. Many have limited obedience to the everyday dos and don'ts of the Old Testament like staying away from fornication or fulfilling your obligations to your church assembly. All these are important things you need to do if you are to stay in righteousness. Yet, that is not all the son is to do. You have been made righteous and empowered to gather the nations (people and land) in Christ Jesus. In the following chapters, we will be looking at practical ways of playing this role. Remember you are not alone. The Holy Spirit is with you. Jesus would have me tell you that He is with you and you will succeed in your assignment.

Chapter 9

VISION AND BOUNDARIES

In the preceding chapters, we have made the vision of God and your part in it clear. Every vision under God has boundaries. God has not called you to do everything. It does not matter if you are alone or belong to a group. If you are doing everything, you are encroaching on someone else's responsibility and not giving your own the hundred percent it needs. If you are the visionary leader, the Holy Spirit may prompt you to train, encourage or employ others to do. Always have it at the back of your mind that you are not called to do it all.

The nature of God is relational. The whole concept of covenant is relationship. God is love. This means every part of God is love. The word love is a relationship word. You will need someone to love otherwise love means nothing.

When someone asked Jesus what was God's most urgent demand from man, Jesus replied that God desired that we loved Him with all of our being and love one another as we love ourselves. God is an 'equal share' God. He also understands that we can only perform according to our ability. He does not value the five talent person above the one talent person. It is what you do with the talent that is important to Him. Use your talent, bear fruit and he will prune you to bear more fruit. God delights in much fruit.

God told Abraham in Genesis 13:14-15 to look up all around him and promised him possession of all the land his eyes could see. That was a very generous offer from a very generous God. Yet there was a limit to how far Abraham's eyes could see. In fact when God brought Israel, the descendants of Abraham, back to possess the promise land, He gave them more than Abraham's eyes could see but set them specific boundaries. The book of Numbers chapter 34, verses 1 to 12 set out specific boundaries. Increase and multiplication is God's business, so as you possess territories, he extends your borders. It is important that your vision has specific geographical boundaries. It helps you to focus and concentrate your abilities.

Our ministry began in the Harlesden area of London. This is a small town. We were originally called Harlesden Christian Fellowship to reflect the boundary of our calling. We functioned as a typical church, taking care of our members and doing the occasional soul winning outreach. The area was dark and had a terrible reputation. We met in an Anglican church hall. The main Anglican church was going to close down because there were just a handful of congregants in this magnificent historical building. The church hall in which we had our services was also the community centre for the area. Three different masonic lodges met there on Saturdays and Sunday evenings. Masonic lodges are self-help fraternities that dabble in ancient pagan rites. The spiritual atmosphere there was dark and I, as the visionary leader, was no spiritual warfare expert.

We had only ten members. In fact I was a reluctant leader of this bunch of rookies. Many of them were friends that I had led to the Lord. I had just been saved three years earlier. These guys would not go to any church. They wanted to stick with me so my pastor released me to lead them. It was a challenging experience in St. Matthew's Church Hall with the karate group or Solomon's Temple lodge waiting at the door to come in as soon as we finished. My vision was not clear. I had been forced into this by my stubborn friends who did not want to come to church with me to be pastored by my pastor. On hindsight I see the hand of God ordering my steps according to his will. God is ready to use any yielded vessel with or without experience.

I did not have to stay in this uncertain state of mind too long. Jesus sorted me out. After attending a meeting by an apostle of God, I could not sleep all night. It was so clear to me that God needed all of Harlesden, and Harlesden needed God.

"Who will go for Me?" God was asking. I could not say no because I didn't know anyone else the question was directed to. I said 'yes'. By saying 'yes', I now had a vision. The vision energised me. Today, I am glad I responded to Jesus. God has extended our boundaries. We are also witnesses of a transformed community. Our area is still 'work in progress' but even the most extreme skeptics will tell you something dramatic has happened in Harlesden and Stonebridge. God be praised. The centre of Harlesden, called Jubilee Clock, has become a preaching rostrum for the many churches that have sprang up in Harlesden. Sometimes, churches queue up to take their turn in openly declaring the saving grace of the Cross of Jesus Christ. As we continue to explore practical ways of fulfilling the will of God, I will bring in examples of some of the challenges we faced and some of the victories we have had. **Have a clear vision with its boundaries.**

Who Is In Your Team?

God's vision for you is always bigger than what you can handle on your own. Some proudly talk about how God has given them a world-wide vision but never go beyond the confines of their churches. Some try to establish branches of their churches in places God has not directed them to. Many do this to satisfy their man-made visions. Some ministries establish branches in richer cities in order to benefit financially. **Any vision that is not God ordained will only bring heartache.** Sometimes, God just calls you to partner with a ministry in that city where you aspire to do business. Do not try to make out a living for yourself. God will handsomely reward you for every effort you put in fulfilling his desire. He will openly reward you for the things you do in secret.

God has an ordained team for every vision. God will never allow you to walk alone. He never walks alone and will not allow you to walk alone. Where the Father is, His Word is and His Spirit is also there. In His throne room, he is constantly surrounded by angels and the 24 elders. He lives inside of you and me. Just as, ideally, every child is born into the waiting arms of loving parents, God prepares a team waiting to partake in the vision. Make the vision known so others who are part of the vision can run with it.

Then the Lord answered me and said:
"Write the vision
And make it plain on tablets,
That he may run who reads it. (Habakkuk 2:2)

When God gave us the vision for Harlesden, we knew we didn't have the capacity or capability on our own to undertake this vision. No church assembly on its own can take a city if there are other assemblies in that city.

I have been in cities where there are several large assemblies but the city remains dark. The reason is one of two: None of the churches has a city-taking vision or the churches there are not working together. Our first step after God gave us the vision was to write to all the churches and let them know the vision God had given to us. Some responded and identified with the vision. Others responded angrily, misinterpreting our letters to mean they were doing nothing. We didn't mean that. Every word of prayer is beneficial to the kingdom. Every little work of God is better than nothing and brings joy to heaven. We therefore ought to respect and honour every genuine ministry for God. The word of God admonishes us to prefer others above ourselves. Our responsibility is to encourage others. Majority of the churches did not respond.

The vision was like fire in our bones so we did not have the option of being discouraged to stall. We decided we would run with those who had expressed interest. As things begun to move we might just draw in those on the fence and hopefully bring in some of the rebels. Please note that some who would promise to go with you are just being 'nice Christians.' They will not turn up. **As long as the vision continues to burn in your heart and you do not give up, the real team will appear.** I do not say this with any sense of triumphalism, but as the vision took shape, the ministers who continued to oppose retired or were transferred and were replaced. We had enthusiastic support from the prayerful Anglican vicar of Stonebridge. God sent a Holy

Spirit filled Anglican bishop to the area who understood spiritual warfare. He developed a fatherly relationship with us. He was an apostle whom God sent to encourage and be a strong pillar for his work in the area. He also appointed spirit filled clergy who were supportive of our work. Others who were previously uninterested crossed the carpet to share in the vision. The Church is the body of Christ and cannot afford to to be disjointed and disunited. I do not suppose any of us would like our bodies to be in disarray. It will affect our head. Jesus Christ is the head and the church is the body. We had a team fully committed to fulfil God's will for our community. At some of our initial joint prayer meetings, there were only 5 of us. We were not discouraged because the vision burnt in our bones. If you are ready for God, he will brand a vision into your soul which cannot be erased.

Help! What Next?

Pray. When you don't know what to do next, just pray. Prayer must precede every step we take. A praying Christian never has a dull moment in life. Fill the time between indecision and action with prayer. When the vision was planted in your heart, you would have prayed before publishing it. You would have been praying whilst getting your team together. Remember the team starts with two. Jesus promises that where two or three are gathered together in His name, he is there with them. It is prayer that will release the rest of the team members. This process could take forever. Yet from the day you said 'yes', God is in business and will continue adding more to your team. Yours is to pray, get direction from the Holy Spirit and obey. **It is prayer that will release strategy for action.** When we started, five ministries committed themselves to meeting fortnightly for prayer for the community. We had an Anglican curate, a London City Mission evangelist, a dear lady prophet who had been praying for the area for years prior to our arrival, a Kensington Temple church plant and us. As stated earlier, there were others who were part of the team but could not make the regular prayer meetings. We honoured them as part of the team and joyfully welcomed them when they could make the meetings.

A movement had started and there was no stopping us. We prayer-walked Harlesden and Stonebridge and identified special targets that we felt were not helping our community and prayed for their removal. We also prayed for more Spirit-filled churches in the area and for God to bless the schools and hospitals and the things that enhanced the community.

When you take a stand as a son of God to bring His will to come to pass on this earth as it is in heaven, you are setting yourself up for war. War needs intelligence and fire power. Prayer will provide both. You are also coming against an enemy who has had unchallenged control of the area for a long time. Prepare yourself for a long drawn out war. If you stand and don't give up, you will be rewarded with victories that will increase your faith and open new doors.

"Finally, my brethren, be strong in the Lord and in the power of His might. Put on the whole armour of God, that you may be able to stand against the wiles of the devil. For we do not wrestle against flesh and blood, but against principalities, against powers, against the rulers of the darkness of this age, against spiritual hosts of wickedness in the heavenly

places. Therefore take up the whole armour of God, that you may be able to withstand in the evil day, and having done all, to stand.

Stand therefore, having girded your waist with truth, having put on the breastplate of righteousness, and having shod your feet with the preparation of the gospel of peace; above all, taking the shield of faith with which you will be able to quench all the fiery darts of the wicked one. And take the helmet of salvation, and the sword of the Spirit, which is the word of God; praying always with all prayer and supplication in the Spirit, being watchful to this end with all perseverance and supplication for all the saints"
(Ephesians 6:10-18)

War needs a concerted effort. If you are with Jesus you are on the winning side. Jesus said after His resurrection that all power in earth and heaven is His. He then commands us to go into the world and make disciples of all nations. We therefore go knowing that we are backed by the ultimate power of God.

Everyone must be part of a bigger vision. You must still have the vision of territory within the bigger vision. God gave Israel their boundaries. Yet within the boundaries, the tribes had their boundaries and within that, families had their boundaries. There is the tendency for people to think they are supporting someone else's vision. An attitude of 'I am only helping' does not bring out the best in you. **It is important that while recognising the bigger vision, you own and tackle the territory apportioned to you as your part of the vision.**

In Harlesden and Stonebridge, we divided the regions into sub regions and assigned each portion to a different church. Some were more effective with their regions than others. We decided to give every household in the area a gift and a gospel booklet as well as invitations to one of our concerts or community barbecues. All the participating churches contributed and purchased thousands of beautiful Jesus key rings and 'Minus to Plus' gospel booklets for every household. We decided to hand deliver and do a door to door follow up. This could only be done by every church covering their territory. Every church that could not cover their territory let the bigger vision down. We ensured that those who were more capable helped those who found it more difficult. Sounds very much like Israel and the promised land. After we discovered a recognisable change in Harlesden and Stonebridge, the Holy Spirit asked us to step up and help take the Borough of Brent. **When you fulfil the little God has given you, He will give you bigger responsibility.** Brent is the local government region of which Harlesden is a part. Greater responsibility is a sign of greater trust from God. We are playing our part together with other ministries in Brent. We were not pioneers. God already had people in place. Brent for Jesus, Assemblies of God and other Christian ministries were already on the ground. We developed strong friendships and understanding which made the work much easier. We are also part of the vision for London, for the United Kingdom and for the World. Play your part, having in mind that your vision is always part of a bigger vision. It is Jesus who is building his church. Just do what he tells you to do.

Chapter 10

CHALLENGES AND VICTORIES

"For My Angel will go before you and bring you in to the Amorites and the Hittites and the Perizzites and the Canaanites and the Hivites and the Jebusites; and I will cut them off. You shall not bow down to their gods, nor serve them, nor do according to their works; but you shall utterly overthrow them and completely break down their sacred pillars.

"So you shall serve the Lord your God, and He will bless your bread and your water. And I will take sickness away from the midst of you. No one shall suffer miscarriage or be barren in your land; I will fulfill the number of your days." I will send My fear before you, I will cause confusion among all the people to whom you come, and will make all your enemies turn their backs to you. And I will send hornets before you, which shall drive out the Hivite, the Canaanite, and the Hittite from before you. I will not drive them out from before you in one year, lest the land become desolate and the beasts of the field become too numerous for you. Little by little I will drive them out from before you, until you have increased, and you inherit the land." (Exodus 23:23-30)

God has made salvation available through His Grace. We are empowered by His Grace. Yet the Father does not want His sons to walk around like wimps sucking our thumbs and expecting honey to drop on our tongues. Jesus has made a public spectacle of Satan and displayed to everyone who cares that the enemy is defeated. Yet He allows Satan to flex his wilted muscles at times so that the sons of God can establish and confirm the authority already given to them by God. Satan and his cohorts will not leave you in peace as you pursue the Father's vision. If you stand your ground and let the Holy Spirit guide you, the victory is sweet.

The main spiritual opponent in Harlesden and Stonebridge was idolatry. Wherever God isn't, your principal opponent is idolatry. The first three commandments to Israel dealt with idolatry. This principality manifests in different forms in different areas. In our area, the main manifestation was false religion. There were several pagan temples in our borough. A black racist group dominated the high street. You would see them every day on the High Street distributing their propaganda leaflets. This group practises their own form of Islam that is anti-white and anti-Jew. They recruit young black boys with a racist agenda. They had a hold over Harlesden. They even owned businesses on the High Street. This, mixed with a few churches going through the motions without the Holy Spirit, made Harlesden a demonic paradise. There was a cult called the Tabernacle of God that had an office and shop in the same office block we operated from. A psychic called Sister Mary had moved unto the High Street.

Where there is idolatry, there is always revelry and sexual immorality. Harlesden was a place associated with sexual vice. One of the most popular rock concert venues in all of London was on our high street. Harlesden was known for drunkenness. The big Guinness factory which produced Guinness for all of the UK and export was on our border. Where the devil has a stamp, you will see the occurrence of several deaths. We experienced this as well in Harlesden. There were so many deaths in a short space of time that we earned the infamous title of "the murder capital of Europe". We were undaunted. We continued to pray and confront these strongholds in the Spirit, confident of God's intervention.

There were a couple of spiritual confrontations worth mentioning. The Nation Of Islam organised a big funeral at Alperton cemetery which I attended. I was there because the parents of the deceased were Baptist deacons who were friends of mine. As the Muslims went through their rituals and seeing a fair number of Christians there, I asked for permission from the chief Imam to say a Christian prayer. My prayer was the cue the Christians needed. After my prayer, what was a Nation of Islam funeral, turned to a Christian celebration. The Christians present were emboldened to sing one gospel chorus after another. You could not stop them and the Muslims were absolutely confused. The atmosphere was completely transformed. I knew we had won a spiritual victory like Elijah at Mount Carmel. We saw the physical manifestation of this victory almost immediately. The Nation of Islam was on a downward spiral. Many of the young men left and to date their influence in the area is at rock bottom.

Another incident was at Roundwood Park where we used to go and pray. There is a hill there which is the highest point in Harlesden so it was a good place for prayer. You could see a good stretch of the town around you and speak into the atmosphere. One day when we arrived for our usual prayer, there was a police presence. Someone had overdosed on drugs and died in a tree at the spot where we prayed. We bound the spirit of death. The family of the boy met us there and asked if after the burial of the young man they could meet us at that spot for a short service. We agreed and had the opportunity to praise the Lord, preach the Gospel and console the family.

The good news is the killings in Harlesden stopped; drug dealers were arrested; Stonebridge estate the 'no go area' has been pulled down and rebuilt. Mean Fiddler, the popular rock joint has closed down; Guinness has closed down its brewing operations; Sister Mary the psychic ran out of town; the leader of the cult Tabernacle of God was found guilty for child molestation in America and the cult has disappeared. The Hindu Temple is still standing but is a shadow of its former self. More Holy Spirit churches have come to Harlesden. The cold churches are hotter with new ministers. God is on a mission to reclaim His world and will succeed. Do you have faith to stand with Him?

Chapter 11

LAST MAN STANDING

The winner in any battle is the one left standing. When Jesus appeared to his disciples after resurrection, he told them he had overcome death, sin, sickness and all that the enemy threw at him. The proof was his being there with them. They saw him on the Cross with all the sin and sickness of the world put on him. They saw his body distorted with all manner of sickness on the Cross. They actually saw him die and buried. Yet there he was in front of them, alive, strong and well. He was the last man standing.

> "O Death, where is your sting? O Hades, where is your victory?" (1 Corinthians 15:55)

The Christian must be built to last. He must be built of material that will last forever. The only one who will last forever is God himself. God therefore offers himself as the construction material of his sons. We are born again by the Spirit of God.

The Beginning and the End

"I am the Alpha and the Omega, the Beginning and the End," says the Lord, "who is and who was and who is to come, the Almighty." (Revelation 1:8).

"And when I saw Him, I fell at His feet as dead. But He laid His right hand on me, saying to me, "Do not be afraid; I am the First and the Last. I am He who lives, and was dead, and behold, I am alive forevermore. Amen. And I have the keys of Hades and of Death." (Revelation 1:17-18).

When my musician friend played his new composition for my appraisal, I inquired about that one note that ran through the song from beginning to the end without a break. He told me that was the 'God note.' God started everything, has always been there and will always be there. Alpha and Omega are the first and last letters of the Greek alphabet. Jesus describes himself as the everlasting; the A to Z of life.

Jesus appeared to John on the Island of Patmos to give him prophetic insight about the end of our time on earth. The book of Revelation is the result of this encounter. John was initially afraid when he saw Jesus. Jesus assured him that he was the last man standing and there was no need to be afraid. If the good and compassionate Jesus is the last man standing and we are in him, then we can be certain of our complete safety. We can be assured of the revelation of his glory in our lives.

"If then you were raised with Christ, seek those things which are above, where Christ is, sitting at the right hand of God. Set your mind on things above, not on things on the earth. For you died, and your life is hidden with Christ in God. When Christ who is our life appears, then you also will appear with Him in glory." (Colossians 3:1-4)

There is no other place of eternal safety except in Jesus Christ. Events will come and go but Jesus will forever be. Your place in him will be your safest place of protection. When Jesus walked the earth as man, his confidence lay in the fact that he knew where he came from, and where he was going. He told his audience that he did not do or say anything except what God, his father, asked him to do. The Jews, who were his audience at the time, found their identity in Abraham and Moses. Their relationship with God was at best, nominal. They worshiped God from a distance. They could therefore not access the strength and life of God. God in his grace would give them signs of his protection when they made a little extra effort towards him. Jesus showed them what it meant to completely abide in God who is from everlasting to everlasting.

Through the death and resurrection of Jesus Christ, the barrier of sin has been removed between us and God. We therefore have full access to God. More than that, we have an invitation to become the sons of God and abide in him forever. Let us respond to this invitation and stay in him forever. A day should not go by that we are not conscious of God's presence in us and our position in Him.

Behold what manner of love the Father has bestowed on us, that we should be called children of God! Therefore the world does not know us, because it did not know Him. Beloved, now we are children of God; and it has not yet been revealed what we shall be, but we know that when He is revealed, we shall be like Him, for we shall see Him as He is. And everyone who has this hope in Him purifies himself, just as He is pure. (1 John 3:1-3).

CHAPTER 12

Final Word

You are blessed to be living in a time like this: 'The Day of the Son' is here. The Son of God has defeated the great adversary, Satan, and paved the way for many sons of God to live the God kind of life. You are chosen to be one of these sons of God. Enjoy your life in the Son as a son. As long as you stay in him, you are safe. He is solidly immovable.

The door of Love, Peace and Fulfilment is wide open.
Grace calls.
Step in, get equipped and have the time of your life.
Submit your will to His will.

Jesus says:

"Come to me, all you who are weary and burdened, and I will give you rest. Take my yoke upon you and learn from me, for I am gentle and humble in heart, and you will find rest for your souls. For my yoke is easy and my burden is light." *(Matthew 11:28-30)*

The blessing of God is with you every step of the way.

www.ingramcontent.com/pod-product-compliance
Lightning Source LLC
Chambersburg PA
CBHW070949080526
44587CB00015B/2238